Sister ♥ Sister ♥ Sister

Getting Along at Full House

By
Jan Berenson

Photo credits:

Cover: Retna, Shooting Star
P. 11, 23: Janet Macoska
P. 38: Ron Galella, Ltd.
P. 44: Shooting Star

Copyright © 1995 Kidsbooks, Inc.
3535 West Peterson Avenue
Chicago, IL 60659

ISBN: 1-56156-393-5

Manufactured in the United States of America

TABLE OF CONTENTS

Page

Introduction: Welcome To *Full House!* 5

Chapter 1: Get To Know JODIE 9

Chapter 2: Meet CANDACE.................... 13

Chapter 3: All About ASHLEY &
MARY-KATE 17

Chapter 4: Behind The Scenes: Oh, Sister! 21

Chapter 5: Getting Along: Jodie & The Olsens;
Candace & Jodie; All Together Now .. 29

Chapter 6: Off Camera: How They're
Different 35

Chapter 7: What They Fight About 41

Chapter 8: Best Friends For Life 45

The *Full House* cast in the
very beginning.

Introduction

WELCOME TO FULL HOUSE!

Full House has been TV's most popular family comedy for seven years. There are many reasons viewers like it so much. Weekly visits with the Tanner family—dad Danny, daughters DJ, Stephanie, and Michelle, plus their live-in relatives and friends—are always heartwarming and fun. Some episodes are very funny, and once in a while, they are sad. But each time, at the end, everyone hugs and feels good all over.

Watching the adorable Tanner sisters grow up is one of the main reasons viewers keep coming back to *Full House*. Each girl has a definite personality all her own, yet they seem exactly like real-life sisters. They may tease each other and fight over silly things, but deep down, they love each other very much.

There's Donna Jo, who is always called DJ. As the oldest sister, she is the responsible one. Sometimes, her little sisters seem like pests, but DJ is there whenever they need her.

Through the years, DJ has grown into a typical teenager. She has her own room and loves to talk on the phone to her friends. She is very interested in boys. For a few years, she had a boyfriend named Steve, but now she dates different guys. Also, DJ is looking forward to going off to college.

Stephanie is the middle sister. She is the witty one, always ready with a funny comeback line. The independent spirit of the family, Stephanie is spunky and honest. She says exactly what's on her mind, even if it gets her into hot water sometimes. Stephanie has grown from a perky five-year-old into a more rebellious preteen. She's spending more time with her friends and starting to like boys.

For a long time, the youngest Tanner was called, "Baby Michelle." When the show first began, she was just eight months old, had a few wisps of hair, and had not begun to walk. But Michelle is not a baby anymore. Over the years, she has learned not only to walk, but to dress herself, go to school, read books, and talk up a storm. Still, Michelle will always be the sweet baby of the Tanner bunch. She is so cute, everyone loves her.

Of course, the Tanners of *Full House* are TV characters. But the young actresses who play them are very real. Candace Cameron is DJ, Jodie Sweetin plays Stephanie, and fraternal twins Mary-Kate and Ashley Olsen have been sharing the role of Michelle since they were babies.

All four girls have grown up on-screen, and become as close as real-life sisters. In this book, you will meet each one of them, and see how they get along when the camera stops rolling. They are as interesting and fun to spend time with as DJ, Stephanie, and Michelle.

At 13, Jodie has blossomed into a
beautiful young teen.

Chapter One

GET TO KNOW JODIE SWEETIN
"Stephanie Tanner"

Jodie's last name describes her perfectly. She is just about the sweetest friend anyone could have. But there's more to this blond-haired bundle of sunshine than just sugar—there's lots of smarts and a dash of spice, too.

Jodie, who is 13 years old, was born in Los Angeles, California. Her parents are Janice and Sam. She has no sisters in real life, and no brothers either. Jodie is an only child.

She started acting at a very young age. "When I was really little, like two or three, people would tell my parents that I should be on TV," Jodie explains. "I guess I was cute or something." Being adorable was not Jodie's only strong suit. "I was kind of a ham," she admits. "I liked to dance and entertain people. I wasn't shy." She was also very smart. She began to talk early and could read children's books at only three years old.

Jodie's parents didn't know anything about show biz. They had no connections. The family had moved to a house over an hour away from Los Angeles. But they decided to let Jodie try out for TV parts and helped her find an agent. It was a good decision. Jodie was successful right away. She was cast in her very first commercial when she was four. It was for hot dogs. She appeared in many more commercials, and then landed her first TV role. No, it wasn't *Full House's* Stephanie. Jodie co-starred in another sitcom called *Valerie*. That show didn't stay on the air very long, but Jodie did such a good job, she was recommended for *Full House*. With her bouncy blond curls and flashing blue eyes, she was perfect for the role of middle daughter Stephanie. "I was the first sister they picked," Jodie says proudly. At the time, she was just six years old.

Being on a TV series changed Jodie's life. She could no longer go to regular school every day with her friends. Instead, she learned her lessons with a tutor on the *Full House* set. She couldn't join school teams or clubs. She had less time to be with her neighborhood pals. But Jodie never felt she

Jodie in her *Full House* dressing room
with one of her favorite Troll dolls.

missed out, for what she got in return was
even better. "I found out what it's like to
have sisters. From the first day I met
Candace, Mary-Kate, and Ashley, we
warmed up to each other. It didn't take us
long to start feeling like a real-life family.
That's really neat."

The early years: cute Candace poses
with older brother Kirk.

Chapter Two
MEET CANDACE CAMERON
"DJ Tanner"

Just like Jodie, Candace's career took off before she started kindergarten. But unlike her TV sister, Candace is not an only child. In fact, it was because of her older brother, Kirk, that she started acting in the first place. Candace is the youngest of Barbara and Robert Cameron's four children. When the kids were small, all of them wanted to be on TV. The Camerons lived just outside Los Angeles in Panorama City. Still, they did not know how to help their children become actors. But their neighbors did. Little Adam Rich used to be on the old TV show, *Eight Is Enough*. Adam's family pointed the way for the Camerons. Before they knew it, freckle-faced Kirk Cameron was the star of TV's hit sitcom *Growing Pains*. Cute Candace was cast in a commercial for an insurance company.

Candace quickly learned the ups and downs of being a child actress. She was all excited, waiting for that first commercial to be aired on TV—only it never did. "My very first commercial got canceled!" she exclaims. Now, she can laugh about it, but back then she was only six, and so disappointed! Still, she bounced back and went on to act in 25 other commercials which did make it to TV. She also landed guest roles on TV's *Punky Brewster* and *St. Elsewhere.*

By the time Candace started grade school, her career was in full gear. So was Kirk's. Unfortunately, her real-life older sisters didn't fare as well. Bridgette and Melissa never did make it as actresses. Sometimes, that made Candace feel bad.

Candace loves to hang out in her dressing room. Here she's with pal Danielle Fishel from *Boy Meets World.*

When *Full House* came along, Candace was 11 years old. Because she'd visited Kirk on the *Growing Pains* set, Candace knew exactly what it would be like to be on a weekly show. It was definitely something she wanted to do! "I knew I liked acting better than doing commercials," she said, "and I saw how much fun Kirk was having. His *Growing Pains* co-stars were like a second family to him. That's what I wanted, too."

Of course, Candace's life changed once she stepped into DJ's Doc Martens. Throughout the years she did commercials, she was able to go to regular school. But after moving into *Full House*, Candace had a private tutor. Although she missed her friends, Candace liked working one on one with her tutor. She also found that she enjoyed being the older sister for a change. "It was weird going from being the baby of the family to acting like the mature one," she admitted, "but I got to like it a lot. Now it feels totally natural."

Ashley and Mary-Kate today—they are superstars!

Chapter Three
ALL ABOUT ASHLEY & MARY-KATE OLSEN
"Michelle Tanner"

The Olsen twins were much too young to remember when they first crawled into show biz. But they've heard the story many times! They were born on June 13, 1986. First came Ashley and then, four minutes later, Mary-Kate arrived. Their parents, Dave and Jarnie Olsen, already had two-year-old Trent at home in Sherman Oaks, a Los Angeles suburb. The twins were not identical, but fraternal. Still, they looked and acted so much alike, it was hard for anyone but their parents to tell them apart. Both girls were sweet, friendly, and simply adorable.

When Ashley and Mary-Kate were six months old, their mom heard about a casting call for twin babies. It was for a show called *Full House.* They were looking for two little girls to share the part of Michelle, the youngest Tanner. That way, if one baby was tired or cranky, the other one could take over in a scene. Viewers would never know the difference.

A friend of Jarnie's ran a talent agency and urged her to bring the babies to the try-out. Of course, Ashley and Mary-Kate couldn't act like anything but what they were—cute, cuddly, and happy twins. That, of course, was enough.

The Olsens made their on-camera debut at the age of one. The girls have done just about everything else on-camera ever since. They've taken their first steps in front of an audience, said their first words, learned to tie their shoes, started preschool, even read their first book.

They never had a problem sharing one role. At first, Ashley used to play Michelle in the scenes where she was active, while Mary-Kate took the quiet scenes. That matched their real personalities. But these days, the twins are such professionals, either one can play any scene at all. They used to repeat their lines after a coach said them. Now, they read their scripts all by themselves.

Spending part of each day with their TV family, and part with their real family, is all they have ever known. Mary-Kate and

Mary-Kate and Ashley with real-life older brother Trent and younger sister Elizabeth

Ashley have never been confused. When they were very little, they used to call their co-stars by their characters' names. Now they no longer do that. They have always thought of everyone on *Full House* as a second family. That has not changed. They love their TV dad, uncle and aunt, and most especially, their older "sisters" Candace and Jodie.

The *Full House* cast has certainly grown.

Chapter Four
BEHIND THE SCENES AT FULL HOUSE: OH, SISTER!

Life behind the scenes at *Full House* is just like a big, bustling, real-life household. As the theme song goes, "everywhere you look, there's a heart, there's a hand to hold on to." Over 100 people report to work there every day! That means there's a constant flow of folks coming and going, greeting each other with, "hi, how are you?" often followed by a friendly peck on the cheek and, of course, a hug.

On TV, the Tanners live in San Francisco. But in real life, *Full House* is taped at a studio in Burbank, California. All the rooms you see—the living room, kitchen, and bedrooms—are all under one roof in a huge two-story building on the Warner Brothers' lot.

Downstairs is the most crowded part of the set. That is where the actors play out their scenes for the show. There is real snack food in the kitchen, a bulletin board with memos and messages tacked on to it, a comfortable couch to flop down on, dozens of cameras, cable wires on the floor, directors and crews to put the show together.

But go up one flight of stairs and the scene is completely different. That's where the dressing rooms are. And that is where you'll often find TV sisters Candace, Jodie, Mary-Kate, and Ashley. It seems just like a real home, with each girl's dressing room next door to the other. Because the girls have grown so close, their doors are open most of the time. It isn't unusual to find Jodie in the twins' room, or all four of them grouped on Candace's couch. They are always going back and forth to borrow something from one another.

Each young actress has decorated her own room. Jodie has pictures of her family and friends on the walls. Since she collects angels and cherubs, there are tiny sculptures all around. On her desk, Jodie piles up her school books. During her breaks, eighth-grader Jodie does her homework at her desk.

Jodie loves to listen to all kinds of music. She's got a huge radio on top of her TV. She's the sister most likely to be blasting the music.

In a quiet moment, Jodie writes letters
to fans and studies her script in her
dressing room.

"If I'm in a loud mood, I'll listen to really loud music, like Nirvana or Green Day," Jodie tells. "If I'm in a relaxing mood, I might find the classical music station." Sometimes, Mary-Kate or Ashley will come in to listen with her even though their favorite music is by the Beach Boys.

The television in Jodie's dressing room gets all the channels, but there's only one she usually watches. That's the special closed-circuit channel where she can view what's going on downstairs on the set. Jodie likes to watch her TV family rehearsing. "It helps me with my own scenes," she explains.

There are all kinds of books scattered around Jodie's room. "I love to read," she says. "My favorite book is *Little Women*, but I also like the *Full House* books about my character Stephanie."

Candace's dressing room has flowered wallpaper, a big couch, two round chairs, and a desk. There are books and magazines, stuffed animals, and framed photos of friends all over. Propped up against the wall is Candace's guitar. She's musically talented, and loves to play and sing for Jodie and the twins. Sometimes, they all sit on the floor in her dressing room, singing along as Candace strums the guitar.

Although each girl has a phone in her dressing room, it's Candace who spends the most time talking. Now 19 years old, she has made many friends that she likes to keep in touch with. But Candace can also be found with her head in a book. She graduated high school and now takes college courses.

Nowadays, Candace leads a very full life. She has a boyfriend, takes classes, and of course, acts on *Full House*.

It isn't surprising that the Olsens' dressing room is the most cluttered. After all, there are two girls sharing one space. Mary-Kate has pictures of horses all around. She loves to go horseback riding, and has even entered riding competitions. "I love horses even more than acting," she tells. Ashley is the ballerina of the bunch. She loves to read books about dancers, and listen to music she can dance to. Ashley collects stuffed monkeys and bears. Many live in her dressing room.

Just like in a real home, there are always parents around at *Full House*. Jodie's mom Janice is good friends with Jarnie Olsen, the twins' mom. They often chat and have coffee together. When Candace was younger, her mom Barbara used to be at *Full House* every day, too. But since Candace turned 18 last year, she looks after herself on the set.

All of the girls look up to Bob Saget, who plays their TV dad, Danny. Tall, gentle, patient, and usually smiling, he is just like a real dad to his TV daughters. He's always there to listen if someone has a problem. He gives them advice and really cares about their interests. When Candace told Bob about a new rock group she wanted to see, he bought her tickets to the concert, and went with her. Bob has been teaching Jodie, Mary-Kate, and Ashley all about computers. "He's such a computer nut," Jodie tells. "He's showed us a lot of things about how the memory works. We mostly play games, like Carmen Sandiego. And he showed us how to make computerized greeting cards and invitations."

Although they have separate tutors, Jodie and the Olsen twins go to school on the *Full House* set. Jodie is a straight-A student. "I love school," she says. "My favorite subject is English. I love to read." Just like a real big sister, Jodie has passed on her love of learning to Mary-Kate and Ashley. The twins are in the third grade now. Ashley loves reading. Mary-Kate's a math wiz.

Sister, Sister, Sister! These girls have a special bond that formed a long time ago.

Chapter Five
GETTING ALONG

JODIE, MARY-KATE, & ASHLEY

As you now know, in real life, Jodie Sweetin is an only child. That's why she loves being on *Full House* so much. She gets to be part of a big family, and have sisters. "The whole cast is great," Jodie bubbles. "It's like having all these uncles and aunts, cousins, brothers, and sisters." She's learned that being part of a large family can have its ups and downs, but that's okay with her, too! "At my real home, it's like there's never anyone waiting for the bathroom, or to use the phone. I never have anybody to fight with, or you know, be like, 'it's my turn to use the phone.' On our show, that's always a problem for somebody. So I get to see what it would really be like having to share."

On *Full House*, Stephanie gleefully teases little sis Michelle. But that's not the case behind the scenes. Jodie has always been close with Mary-Kate and Ashley. "I love little kids," she explains. Jodie has always acted exactly like a real-life big sister to the Olsens. "When they were really small, I used to teach them the alphabet, and play school activities and games with them. Now that they're older, I can just talk to them. We spend a lot of time together, just hanging out and talking. They're so sweet!"

Jodie, Mary-Kate, and Ashley love
hanging out together.

CANDACE & JODIE

Although Candace loves being part of *Full House*, she didn't need the show to experience what life is like in a large family. As you know, Candace is the youngest of the four Camerons. Her family has always been especially close-knit. She learned about acting from big brother Kirk. She grew up sharing a room with Melissa. She has always been able to go to both Bridgette and Melissa for sisterly advice about everything—from friends, to school, to clothes, makeup, hairstyles, and of course, boys.

Candace learned how to be an older sister from Bridgette and Melissa. That is why she knows how to act like one to Jodie and the twins. Now she knows just what to say when the younger girls come to her for advice. When the show first began, Candace was 11 and Jodie was six. They used to play board games together and share secrets. Candace now has less time to hang out with Jodie, because she's busy with her college studies and her own social life. Candace also has a steady boyfriend.

But there is still much that the girls share. Candace and Jodie are both devoted to helping other people, especially children who are sick, or need help. Candace has been active in the Starlight Foundation and Make-A-Wish charities. Her own family runs a week-long summer camp for seriously ill children. Candace speaks out against drug and alcohol abuse. She thinks it's important to set a good example for her young fans. "Kids look up to me, and that's cool," she says.

Jodie has taken a cue from her TV big sis. She has helped raise money for Juvenile Diabetes research. She has granted wishes to seriously ill children whenever she is called upon. As she gets older, Jodie looks forward to following in Candace's caring footsteps.

ALL TOGETHER NOW

Because Candace, Jodie, Ashley, and Mary-Kate have practically grown up together, they can usually tell what the others are thinking. Sometimes, they don't even have to talk to communicate. They've developed a "secret" language all their own. It could be a certain way they look at each other, or a silly signal. Jodie always knows what Candace means when she rolls her eyes. Ashley can tell when Jodie's about to burst out laughing. They tell jokes that no one else gets. "We act weird all the time," Jodie giggles.

When Jodie celebrated her 13th birthday with a big party at Disneyland, her entire *Full House* family was invited. Everyone came, including, of course, Candace and the Olsens!

While other young performers often invite outside friends to come and visit them on the set, Candace, Jodie, Ashley, and Mary-Kate rarely do. "We have each other—and that's enough," they all agree.

When she's not acting, Jodie is just a regular teenager who likes swimming, talking on the phone, and boys!

Chapter Six

OFF CAMERA: HOW THEY'RE DIFFERENT

All four girls agree that as TV sisters, they have the best of both worlds. They get to spend a lot of time together, but they get to go home when they've had enough of each other. After all, each girl is an individual and very much her own person. When TV's Tanner girls do return to their real-life homes after the show, they pursue their separate interests.

Candace Cameron is very different from DJ, the character she plays. Although she is as close as can be with her family, she no longer lives with them. Last year, Candace purchased her own home. She now has a house all to herself and her dog, Sydney. On the days she doesn't work at *Full House*, Candace goes to college. At night, she often hangs out with her sisters Bridgette and Melissa.

For fun, Candace plays tennis and goes horseback riding. She goes to rock concerts with her friends. Her favorite bands are Jodeci, Counting Crows, and Hootie and the Blowfish.

Staying healthy and in good shape is very important to this young actress. Candace has a gym set up at home and she works out every single day.

When she was in high school, Candace used to date boys every once in a while. Now, she has her first steady boyfriend. He is a professional hockey player named Valery. Although Valery is often on the road with his team, he and Candace see each other as often as they can. "Going out to a quiet dinner is our favorite thing to do," she says.

Although she is one of the most popular young stars on TV, Candace is a very low-key person. Watching her brother's career has taught her a very important lesson. Kirk used to be a very popular teen star, and then his career faded. From that, Candace learned that the most important thing in life is not being a TV star, but having a family who loves you. In Candace's case, she happens to have two families— and sisters on all sides!

Jodie Sweetin lives with her mom and dad in a small town outside of Los Angeles.

When she doesn't have to be in L.A. for *Full House,* she rarely heads into the big city. She prefers to join her friends at school and get back into the swing of things with them. "My best friend is Tia and I go over her house all the time," Jodie reports. "Or we'll be talking on the phone." Because she's so sweet and friendly, Jodie has a lot of friends. They are not jealous that she is on TV. "They don't bug me," she tells. "They just might say, 'Oh, I saw *Full House* last night, it was good.' Then they just go back to treating me like a normal person."

When she's with her best buds, Jodie likes to go bike riding or swimming. She has friends who are boys, but no romantic boyfriend. "I like guys as friends more," she tells, "but sometimes they act immature. I can't stand that."

Although Jodie considers Mary-Kate and Ashley two of her best friends, she doesn't usually see them off the set. But sometimes, the two families vacation together. "We went on a trip to Big Bear, California last year," Jodie says. "We baked cookies and had a picnic. It was fun."

Sometimes, Jodie just likes quiet time all to herself. That's when she'll most likely read a book, or sit down and listen to music. In those quiet hours, Jodie realizes how lucky she is. She has great friends and two loving families, on and off camera.

Ashley and Mary-Kate Olsen live in a full house in real life, too. In their family, they are the middle sisters. Their older brother Trent is now 10. They have a younger sister named Elizabeth, who is five. The family lives just outside Los Angeles. Each girl has her own bedroom. Ashley's has white wallpaper with white and pink flowers on the borders. She has five stuffed monkeys and over 50 stuffed teddy bears in her room. Mary-Kate's room also has flowered wallpaper. She has a wooden horse with a saddle in her room.

Mary-Kate and Ashley love their
"superstar" chairs.

When the twins aren't at *Full House*, they go to regular school. They are not in the same class there, and they have different friends. Their friends have no trouble telling them apart. They know that Mary-Kate has a round face and Ashley has an oval one.

Ashley and Mary-Kate don't dress alike when they are in school. Ashley likes her clothes loose and baggy. Mary-Kate prefers some things tight and other things loose. The girls have different interests. Mary-Kate is the big animal lover. She especially loves horses and takes riding lessons. "I used to ride western saddle—that's the one with the horn in front—but now I ride English," she explains. Mary-Kate proudly displays the ribbons she's won in competitions on her wall.

Ashley's three favorite things are reading, dancing, and playing computer games. She also takes ballet lessons.

Even though Ashley and Mary-Kate star in a TV show, they don't watch much at home. They don't even watch *Full House*! They like to rent videos instead. *The Blue Bird* is the name of Ashley's favorite video. "It's about a bird that needs to be taken care of," she tells. Mary-Kate's favorite videos include *Black Beauty* and *Andre, The Seal.* The girls like to play video games on the computer, too. They don't have a computer at home, but at school they do. *Reader Rabbit* is the one Ashley is best at.

The Olsens like being twins. They say that the best part is never being lonely. "You always have someone to play with." Of course, there is always someone to fight with, too. The girls argue over clothes and toys. "We're always saying, 'This is mine! No, it's mine,' " Ashley admits.

In their real-life family, Mary-Kate and Ashley are big sisters to Elizabeth. They call her Liz. They have taught her many things. Sometimes, Liz comes to watch her big sisters playing Michelle on *Full House.* Liz wants to be an actress, too. She will appear in the twins' new video called *Mystery At Sea.*

In some ways, Mary-Kate and Ashley are just like Michelle. But unlike her, they are lucky enough to have two families. They get to be younger sisters on TV, and older sisters at home.

Chapter Seven
WHAT THEY FIGHT ABOUT

Just like real sisters, there are times when TV's Tanner girls get annoyed with each other. They don't compete for boyfriends, or for more funny lines on the show. And because they don't really live together, they don't fight over chores or possessions. But they have been known to bicker over silly things. Someone may have forgotten to return a book, or a favorite sweater. Someone else may be playing the music too loud in her dressing room when one of the other girls is trying to study. There are always times when someone's having an off day and keeps tripping over her lines, forcing re-takes. That ticks people off, too.

It took time for Jodie, Mary-Kate, and Ashley to accept that Candace has grown up. She doesn't hang around the set as long as she used to with her TV sisters when she's finished working. And when she is

Jodie can't stay angry at her *Full House* sisters for very long.

there, she spends time on the phone with her boyfriend. Candace doesn't share all her secrets with her younger TV sisters anymore. Of course, that is normal, even for real-life sisters.

Jodie and Candace wouldn't be human if every once in a while they didn't feel a tinge of jealousy over the attention Mary-Kate and Ashley get. There was a time when folks were saying that the Olsen twins were the stars of *Full House.* That had to make the others feel a little left out. But because they love their TV sisters, they've long gotten over that. Instead of feeling envious, they are as proud as big sisters could be.

Mary-Kate and Ashley will surely be superstars for some time!

Candace wants to remain cozy on the homefront for now.

Someday Jodie may be Broadway bound!

Chapter Eight
BEST FRIENDS FOR LIFE

Candace, Jodie, Mary-Kate, and Ashley have played sisters for seven years. That's a long time! They have shared secrets, giggles, and sometimes tears. They have had experiences together that no one else could possibly understand. For that reason, these four young actresses will always have a strong bond.

Jodie Sweetin has had the best of two worlds. She's been able to balance a successful career with a fun private life and that's exactly what Jodie hopes to keep on doing!

Jodie started in show biz before she was really old enough to know why she liked it. Now, she does. Jodie has discovered that she really loves acting and wants to get better at it. She wouldn't mind starring in a new TV series, or even being in a movie. But Jodie has a secret dream, too. She has taken dancing lessons for many years and recently started singing lessons. "My dream is to perform in musical theater," she tells. You can bet when that day comes, all her family will be in the opening night audience—including her TV sisters.

Candace is the Tanner sister who just may take a break from acting. Of the sisters, she's been doing it the longest—13 years! During that time, she has not only played DJ on *Full House*, but guest-starred in other shows as well. Candace has also made many TV movies. She is the sister who showed Jodie how to happily balance being an actress with being a normal kid. All during her junior high and high school years, Candace kept in contact with her regular friends. She knew the importance of getting an education and earning good grades. One semester, Candace even went to Spain as an exchange student.

Now, she wants to take more classes in college. She also wants to travel and see different parts of the world. Music is an important part of her life, and Candace would like to get better at playing the guitar and singing. Getting married and having a family is another one of her dreams. Candace's brother Kirk got married at a young age. He and his wife are very happy together. Candace herself may not announce wedding plans quite that soon, but when she does, you can guess who will be on top of the guest list—three people who have shared her life—Jodie Sweetin and Mary-Kate and Ashley Olsen.

The Olsen twins are most likely to stay squarely in the spotlight. Although they were babies when they first started, both twins have grown to love performing. They never want to stop. They have plans to make many more videos, records, TV specials, and TV movies. They may also star in a brand-new TV series. They won't share the same role as they do now, but they will play twin sisters instead.

This summer, Mary-Kate and Ashley will be the stars of a new movie. It is a comedy called *Double Trouble*. It is the story of twins who grew up with different families. They meet accidentally and change places. Guess who they'll invite to the premiere? There's no doubt Jodie Sweetin and Candace Cameron will be there!

Everyone in the cast of *Full House* is proud to be a part of it. "It has always sent a positive message, and we will all come away with good feelings about the show," says Candace.

The sisters will always have good feelings about each other, too. A special place in each of their hearts will forever be reserved for the others. And no matter where each one goes from here, they will never be more than a phone call away. The kind of love and support they feel is the kind that lasts forever. Indeed, no matter where Candace, Jodie, Ashley, and Mary-Kate go, everywhere they look, there really will always be "a heart, and a hand to hold on to." In a very real way, they'll always be sisters.

WHERE YOU CAN WRITE: To say "hi" or for some "sisterly" advice, drop a note to Candace, Jodie, or the Olsen twins c/o *Full House*, ABC-TV, 2040 Avenue of the Stars, Los Angeles, CA 90069.